99 & STILL IN BUSINESS

Proven Principles for Business Success

WILLIAM H. GARRISON

Copyright © 2020 William H. Garrison

All Rights Reserved.

ISBN: 9798644763566

Legal Notice

This book is copyrighted by the Author and all rights are expressly reserved worldwide. No part of this book may be reproduced or transmitted in any form or any means, electronic or mechanical, including recording, photocopying or by any type of information storage or retrieval system, without getting permission in writing from the Author and Publisher.

The publication contains the opinions and ideas of its author and is designed to provide useful advice to the reader on the subject matter covered. Any references to any products or services do not serve as an endorsement or recommendation. The Author and Publisher strive to be as accurate and complete as possible in the creation of this book, but do not guarantee that the information or suggestion will affect everyone who reads it. The Author and Publisher disclaim any responsibility for any liability, losses or damages of any kind as a consequence, directly or indirectly arising from the use and/or application of any content of this book.

Reading this book does not equal or serve as a substitute for cognitive therapy, clinical counseling, professional advice-giving, mental health care, or treatment for substance abuse. The Author and Publisher are not functioning as licensed mental health professionals, and use of this book is not intended as a quick replacement for counseling, psychiatric interventions, treatment for mental illness, recovery from past abuse, professional medical advice, legal counsel, financial assistance or other professional services.

Dedication

This book is dedicated to Hazel, my wife of 74 years, who was my treasured life and business partner and a constant inspiration to me.

CONTENTS

A Word from the Author 1

Foreword 3

Principle 1: Accept Responsibility 6

Principle 2: Hard Work Pays Off 15

Principle 3: Cultivate A Support System 21

Principle 4: Make A Good Impression 33

Principle 5: Look For Skills And Ability 42

Principle 6: Employee Incentives Work 47

Principle 7: Don't Run From Risks 57

Principle 8; Confront Problems Head-On 65

Principle 9: Stay Humble 73

Principle 10: Never Give Up 82

Bonus: Necessity is the Mother of Invention 90

Bonus: James and Bootsie 95

Epilogue 99

A Word from the Author

I can state without any mental reservation that I have lived my life fully and without limitation. While it hasn't been a perfect life or a problem-free life, it has been a productive one. In my lifetime, I have had the good fortune to own several businesses under the name Garrison Industries, Inc. All of the companies were in the steel industry and were very successful.

Even at my advanced age, the whole idea of retirement seems very foreign to me. In my way of thinking, retirement always meant exchanging the workplace for a rocking chair. For me, the rocking chair is a reminder that your next place just might be the cemetery!

In all honesty, what gets me up in the morning is having something meaningful to do. I have always enjoyed being busy and having some type of project. I have worked hard all of my life. I think part of the reason why I have lived so long is that I have kept my mind and body active. I have always been engaged in some kind of work or project. My philosophy has been that if you work hard at something, you will most likely have a higher chance of success than if you don't.

As I think about my adult daughters and adult grandchildren and what the future looks like for them, I feel quite concerned. If we don't get rid of our pervasive entitlement mentality and non-caring attitude, then I am not sure what the future holds for this great country.

Foreword

Some may question why I wrote a book about entrepreneurship in my late 90's. Many would think that the events and circumstances that I experienced have little practical value in the global marketplace where machines and technology have taken over the work once done by humans. Some may also believe the opportunities to start a small business are almost nonexistent. A young man's or woman's dream of owning their own business has faded into pursuing advanced educational degrees or a high-paid position in an international corporation. To those skeptics, I say, *"that couldn't be further from the truth!"* OR *"you are wrong!"*

While the physical environment that we live in has certainly changed from the neighborhoods and cities of my youth, people remain the same. The anxiety for those born between 1920 and 1945 - the Silent Generation - was just as high as those faced by the Millennial Generation today. Back then the worries of a world at war differ little from those of a world devastated by the coronavirus in 2020. I believe that young people today are not much different in their ambitions, capabilities, or resilience than my generation or the generations before me.

The wisdom and experience of my elders were the foundation of my business success and, more importantly, the happiness and satisfaction I have enjoyed during my life. My thoughts and experiences in this book are my contributions to those courageous entrepreneurs who believe in their dreams and that they can still make a difference in their lives.

In the ups and downs of owning businesses with both successes and failures, I believe I have learned some things that do and don't work. While I understand that there are many changes and advances in technology, I still think there are timeless principles that work. I believe these principles work no matter the business or industry. My hope is that some of the wisdom I have gained throughout my life in owning and operating companies will be helpful to you and your future success.

PRINCIPLE 1

Accept Responsibility

"The price of greatness is responsibility."

— **Winston Churchill**

Why do some people feel that they are owed more than others? The shopper with a cart full of groceries ignores the sign limiting the aisle for those with ten items or less. Teenagers muscle into lines in front of those who have been patiently waiting. Smokers ignore "No Smoking" signs. People feel they are entitled to everything without regard to how others are affected.

This thinking is so different from the era in which I grew up. Times were hard in the Depression era - the 1920s and 1930s - unemployment was at 40%, but there were no entitlements of any kind. We had little, sometimes just enough to get by; other times, not even that. Yet we appreciated everything we had. People in today's world seem to want to get something for nothing and don't enjoy anything.

It seems to me that responsibility and self-pride are two sides of the same coin. If I take care of myself and my family, no one else is burdened with their care. In fact, I may have enough to help others who may not be as fortunate. I help others, not because I must or they are entitled to my help, but as part of the community we share.

In times past, people seemed to be more united and focused on helping each other and practicing the

Golden Rule (*love your neighbor as yourself*). In my day, it wasn't uncommon to see neighbors talking to one another, hanging out on their front porches and yards spending time together. Today, people hardly take the time to learn the first names of their neighbors, People barely even speak to one another. I am not surprised that the cases of depression and suicide have become common in cities and towns across the country.

I recently heard that around 90 years ago, 90% of American adults participated in or attended church. I also grew up going to church. Most people went to church, and communities came together to help one another. Being part of a church fostered a sense of belonging and community. Currently, only about 15% of the population attends church regularly. That is a sad reality to me, and I wonder what it means for the future?

I know that some people are born with an advantage while others get the short end of the stick. That is and will always be the situation. Each person has a choice. They can spend their lives complaining and blaming, being eternally unhappy, always looking for a scapegoat. Or they can resolve to overcome the obstacles they face and make a new path to the future.

Many, many men and women have overcome the limitations of their birth and upbringing:

- Helen Keller was born blind and deaf. Even so, she graduated Phi Beta Kappa from Radcliffe College, the first with her disabilities to do so.

- Walt Disney was raised on a small farm and barely was able to make ends meet. He started off drawing pictures to sell to his neighbors. He was often jobless because no one would hire him. So, his brother had to help him get work. He once had a newspaper editor fire him and tell him that he "had no imagination." He eventually started animating his own cartoons which led to television, movies, and theme parks. At the time of his death, Walt Disney was a multi-millionaire.

- Ella Fitzgerald lived on the streets of New York City, after her mother's death, and struggled greatly until she entered and won an amateur singing contest and became an American icon.

- Arnold Schwarzenegger lived without plumbing or a phone while growing up in a post-World War II Austrian town. There were food shortages and riots occurring outside his door regularly. He made his mind up to become the best bodybuilder in the world, worked extremely hard, and succeeded. He went on to become one of Hollywood's biggest actors and eventually was elected as the Governor of California.

- In 1956, high school dropout Alan Gerry made the decision to take the $1,500 he earned from a small business and start a cable company. The company went on to become known as Cablevision, which sold to Time Warner for an estimated $2.7 billion in 1996.

I didn't always have support in my life. In fact, you could say that how I grew up was far from supportive, and my family was a challenge at best! I had one brother and also a sister who died at 8 months with spinal meningitis. My mother passed away when I was just four years old. As you can imagine, at such a young age, this was highly devastating to me!

My father remarried a much younger woman who bore 5 more children. To me, life seemed very unfair and cruel. Not only was it hard to accept this woman as my new mother, but I also had a father who had anger and rage issues. I remember him repeatedly telling me that I would never amount to anything.

During those tumultuous years, I ran away from home several times because I wanted to leave that situation as soon as I could.

For me, having a difficult family wasn't the end of my story. Despite hardships and battles in life, I learned to make decisions about what I really wanted. In many ways, my father's negative words were the fuel for me to do something with my life and prove him wrong!

Growing up as I did, I adopted a strong work ethic and created a determination to survive and succeed. Most people think challenges or even hard times are their enemies and unfair, but I believe the exact opposite is true. I have always believed that hardships can build character. This was the message I always gave my children and grandchildren, and it was definitely one that I lived and experienced throughout my life.

If you want something, whether it is in life or business, there are generally no shortcuts to getting it. Don't expect anyone else to do it for you or to rescue you. The buck stops with you, always. You are in charge and in the driver's seat of your life. At the end of the day, life and people don't owe you anything. When you think about it, we are not even entitled to the life we live. It is a gift.

So, my first principle of business success is to take responsibility for your business. Take pride in yourself and what you do. Care about yourself and others.

PRINCIPLE 2

Hard Work Pays Off

"I am a great believer in luck, and the harder I work, the more I have of it."

— Thomas Jefferson

What concerns me most about today's world is that many people don't seem to want to work. If hard work is involved, they immediately seek out something easier. I'm always surprised when I go to a business, store, or restaurant, and people are barely just doing the minimum to get by. Their absence of effort and poor attitude signals a lack of pride in themselves, their employer, and the customers they serve.

I suspect that people who shirk work, expecting others to care for them, have always been around. More than 3,000 years ago, King Solomon, the author of the Old Testament's Book of Proverbs, wrote, *"In all toil there is profit, but mere talk tends only to poverty."* At the end of the 19th century, Thomas Edison recognized that *"There is no substitute for hard work."* His friend, Teddy Roosevelt, wrote that he pitied *"the creature who does not work."* Their observations are as correct today as when they were written.

Newspaper columnist Ann Landers once said, *"Opportunities are usually disguised as hard work, so most people don't recognize them."* I live by that. You work hard so you can play hard. At the end of the day, you put the work in, and over time it pays off. It could be in a year or it could be in 10 years. Eventually, your hard work will reward you.

It is quite a thing reflecting over my past and comparing it to how it is now. In many ways, our lives have been made easier because of our modern conveniences and technology. However, despite our conveniences and technological advancements, the principle of hard work still holds true.

When I was 18 years old, I was employed as a helper to a combination welder at a paper mill of 4,000 employees. Around 400 of them were maintenance personnel in various trades.

Welding is hot, physical, and dangerous work, especially when done on an industrial site. On my first day, the department manager warned the new employees that they must be able to replace their mechanic when he was unavailable. Anyone who couldn't comply would be fired. I worked hard and learned a lot from the mechanic I assisted. Fortunately, he was an exceptional craftsman, capable of welding almost any type of metal with any kind of equipment in any position.

Interestingly, he told me that he had never solved the problem of welding white metal (pewter). The difficulty was due to the low melting temperature of 600 degrees. The heat of the torch, without extreme care and extraordinary patience, would melt pewter and make it run like water.

Near the end of my second work anniversary, one of the foremen brought a broken measuring tool to the welding shop for repair. It was essential to operations, in constant use, to measure the length of paper rolls. The device also contained pewter, so none of the senior welders would attempt to repair it because of the difficulty of welding it.

As a 20-year-old, I volunteered to try. Looking back, I am not sure if I was really stupid or really overconfident. This was a big risk for the paper mill executive who accepted my offer and also for me. If I failed, each of us could have lost our jobs. However, not trying was not an option. Without the tool, the plant would have been shut down, costing the plant about $100,000 a day until it could be replaced. Besides, I felt that I could do the job because of the hours I had spent listening and learning from my mentor. I practiced until I was sure I had mastered the skill.

I will never forget how happy the representative was when we were successful! I was too! A few days later, the supervisor promoted me, and I earned top pay.

This outcome was the result of my confidence gained by two years of hard work and my willingness to step up to the challenge. That incident occurred almost 80 years ago, and I never again needed to weld pewter metal since then.

I was fortunate to learn as a young man that the number one key to any kind of success is to not be afraid to work hard and actually expect to work hard. Get busy, roll up your sleeves, and work hard in your endeavors. Get up and make things happen every day. I promise that you will have a higher chance of succeeding if you do!

PRINCIPLE 3

Cultivate A Support System

"Great things in business are never done by one person. They're done by a team of people."

— Steve Jobs

The life of an entrepreneur is not a bed of roses and easy riches. It would be nice if it was that way, but it is not. Instead, it is a career filled with stress, setbacks, and failures. For every moment of success, there are times when you struggle with doubt and disappointments. Where the buck stops is a lonely place with no one to share the psychological burden of leadership.

Most entrepreneurs experience crises of faith - times when they wonder if the goal will be achieved. Will there be enough money to complete the job? Did I bid a job too tight to make money? Will someone beat me to the market? Business owners often have many sleepless nights of worry.

Wives and Families

Entrepreneurs are typically extreme optimists and exceptionally self-confident, two traits that are essential to making a dream reality. They sometimes forget that others - wives and families - experience the same experiences as the entrepreneur, except they have no control over outcomes. They are passengers, not the driver, on the entrepreneur's journey.

While I have been given credit for my success, it would not have happened without the continued, unwavering support of my wife and family. As I began my career, the best thing I ever did in life was marrying a beautiful Christian lady on Valentine's Day in 1946. My wife Hazel was a tremendous support to me in my life and my business endeavors.

She was brilliant. The year we married, she applied for a regional manager's position with the Veterans Administration within the State Capital Building in Columbia, South Carolina. All of the candidates were required to take a pre-employment I.Q. test. She passed with flying colors with a score of 160, forty points above the high normal. The person who monitored the test later told me that she had the highest score ever recorded in that building.

More importantly, Hazel was devout in her faith, what some people would call a "CHRISTIAN in capital letters." She always demonstrated more concern for others than herself. I definitely married well. Not only was she smart, but she was a kind and loving person. She was also an incredible help and support to me in my business endeavors and a critical key to my success. I also have two daughters, two grandchildren, and three great-grandchildren, all very gifted with great potential. They have been an enormous support to me in the past and even now.

Learning Experiences and Mentors

Learning experiences are also invaluable. In 1948, I was hired as an erection superintendent for field construction projects for a large steel manufacturing and fabricating company in Norfolk, Virginia. My first assignment was to erect two 6-million-gallon water tanks for a municipal waterworks in Virginia. The tanks were 187 feet in diameter and 42 feet tall. A completed tank required six circular bands of steel plates, each band measuring 84 inches by 25 feet. Each plate was 7 feet wide by 25 feet long. The bottom ring was made of plates 1 3/8 inches thick and weighed 10,000 lbs. each. Each of the other five rings was reduced in gauge by ¼ inch and the top ring was ¼ inch thick. Altogether, we had to work with more than 300 of those massive plates. It was quite a project and took six months with 30 welders to complete. At the time, the tanks were the largest in the country to be erected.

Another project in Virginia was at Kerr Dam in Bassett, Virginia to install three water tubes from the river bottom to the top of, 270 feet height erected on a vertical 30 degree angle. Two tubes were 9 feet in diameter, one tube was 4 feet in diameter.

My next assignment was to fabricate and erect a 1,100 m.ph. wind tunnel at Langley Air Base in Hampton, Virginia. I often wondered what the tunnel would be used for. In 1963 while reading a local state paper, I read about the wind tunnel being used in the Apollo Space program 50 years earlier.

Other learning experiences for me were my contract jobs and field assignments in North Carolina, Georgia, Florida, and Virginia. On these jobs I had crews of men who traveled with me and they were highly skilled individuals. When we arrived on any job site, we were in place and working within just two hours. We did power plant additions, asphalt stills, and fuel storage tanks.

What I learned and experienced in my various supervisory field experiences was invaluable to me. However, any learning curve can definitely be shortened by having a good mentor. The old expression *"you don't know what you don't know"* is so true. Sometimes, we fail because we simply lack information or experience. Without both, we do not have the knowledge to analyze for a decision, nor the wisdom to make the right choices. Mentors are invaluable to an entrepreneur as well as great teammates. Both should be part of a functioning support system.

Fortunately for me, the 87-year-old chairman of the company I worked for, Gary Steel, reached out to me. Mr. Gary, Sr. and I became friends as well as mentor-student. Our first meeting was life-changing and one of the most valuable relationships of my life. I attribute my later success in the steel business to him.

Even though he had a PhD in engineering and also taught engineering at Virginia Tech before I was born, my mentor was gentle and humble. There were no diplomas, awards, or pictures hanging on his office walls to suggest his education or many accomplishments.

One day, while visiting his office, I noticed a small 8-inch square plaque on his desk that read, *"Nothing ever happens around here important enough to lie about."* When I mentioned how much I admired the note on his desk, he thanked me and gave me a copy of a printed engineering handbook that he had just completed. The 150 pages of formulas and calculations collected over his lifetime was an essential resource for me throughout the rest of my career.

In 1952, while still employed with the same steel company, I transferred to North Carolina to build and manage a new plant to manufacture 5,000-gallon aircraft refueling transport trailers for the U.S. Navy. These trailers were manufactured and shipped to Korea.

Soon after I began construction of this new plant, Mr. Gary, Sr. would travel over 100 miles each week from Norfolk to Rocky Mount to assist me in equipping the new plant. He was 89 at the time. One day, he asked, *"Do you know exactly how the plant should be wired, so equipment can be moved without electrical assistance?"* When I said I did not, he invited me to join him at a drawing board where he drew a sketch of what was needed and what I should expect from the electrical contractor. The old gentleman had a marvelous ability to teach. Our time together was an incredible learning experience. He was a mentor and friend who helped me to successfully design and build the plant. I learned more from that man than I could have ever received from years of formal education.

When it comes to success, mentors are invaluable. What you don't know, you don't know. An essential key to success is being open to learning new things. Find a great mentor and they will be invaluable to your success. A mentor can exponentially hasten the learning curve for you. This was very true for me.

I learned a long time ago that you are only as good as the people who surround you. People that have achieved success will tell you that it had a lot to do with the people they had on their team or in their corner. Few entrepreneurs have success relying solely on themselves. Everybody needs help from time to time, even if it is nothing more than a tap on the shoulder to say, *"I still believe in you."* And success is so much sweeter when shared with those who mean the most.

Whether it is family, friends, or employees, you need people you can count on to be there for you. We are always better… together!

PRINCIPLE 4

Make A Good Impression

"You never get a second chance to make a first impression".

— **Will Rogers**

Psychologists claim that people form opinions about a new acquaintance within 3 to 10 seconds of meeting them for the first time. Are they friend or foe? Are they necessary to achieving my goals? Can I trust them?

Wrong first impressions are difficult to change. Humans do not like to change their minds and go to extraordinary lengths to find information that reinforces their first impression. Whether an opinion based on a first impression is fair or not, its impact on a future relationship is indisputable.

Throughout a career, an entrepreneur will create hundreds of first impressions with potential investors, lenders, employees, customers, vendors, and suppliers. In each case, the outcome will depend on the other party's favorable opinion of the entrepreneur and his company. With so much at stake, I have often wondered why some people sabotage their own interests with inappropriate appearance, language, or bad manners? Is it a lack of awareness or do they just not care?

Appearance

Styles have certainly changed since I began my business career. In the 1950s and 1960s, most men were clean-shaven and worked in an office wearing a suit, a starched white shirt, and tie as well the ultra-shined shoes polished each Saturday or Sunday night. Women wore knee-length dresses with high heels and, sometimes, a hat. Working men wore freshly pressed khaki pants and shirts to and from work, occasionally switching to older garments if they worked in a factory. Men wore hats and always removed them indoors.

During the 60s, dress standards began to grow casual. Suits and ties were replaced with sports coats and open shirts. Barbershops with their traditional red and white striped poles changed to mall salons with stylists. Flattops grew to coiffured mops and pony-tails (on men), and beards of all shapes and lengths flourished. The hems of women's skirts rose well above the knee, and modesty gave way to flaunting.

About that time, we made a family trip to Quebec, Canada. What a vivid contrast between the way people dressed in Quebec and the cities of America. Walking through the airport in New York City, I felt like I had returned to "Tee-Shirt City". It is even worse today. People slouch around half-dressed, men's pants sagging down, women wearing outfits more suitable for the bedroom or beach than the street, and I think to myself, *"What happened? Do people not care how they look? Am I living in some kind of third-world country?"*

Most people do not recognize the impact of their looks on other people. A brilliant young computer programmer with a whisker-stubble and wrinkled, dirty clothes asking for a loan might not realize that a banker is more likely to equate his slovenliness with his work production. Visible tattoos or body piercings might be overlooked by friends. However, potential investors are more likely to associate body art with rebels and someone who may not work well with others.

When choosing what to wear for meeting someone the first time, consider the meeting environment and the dress of the person you will meet. For example, most bankers, lawyers, and corporate executives wear suits and ties; small company owners might dress more casually. Do your homework first, then choose the apparel that makes your clothes a non-issue.

Recently, an acquaintance stopped me on the street and asked me why I was so dressed up? *"I am going to my own funeral,"* I replied with a smile. Of course, I was joking, but her question was a sign of the times. The real reason I take the time to look my best, no matter what the day holds for me, is that little details like your appearance matter. How I look totally influences my mindset for the day. If I don't care about my appearance, my attitude may carry over into everything else I do that day.

Language

First impressions are also given by the language we use. If I call someone in customer service and talk to a rude or impatient person on the other end of the phone, then I may not be so inclined to continue the conversation. Or, if the individual murmurs or doesn't speak distinctly, I form an immediate negative impression about that company.

Words matter. Words and subjects that were once considered taboo in polite society are common today in conversation, television, and the movies. "Rough" language, once the purview of men doing physical labor, is mainstream with men and women. However, no one should assume that everyone accepts or is comfortable with today's lack of speech boundaries.

Using crass language might be acceptable in a private conversation with friends or between workers in a factory or on a job site. However, those same words would be inappropriate in a business meeting or an interview. The words we speak and the subjects we discuss create an impression of who we are as much as our appearance does.

Manners

The manners we follow reflects the way we speak to and treat others. Good manners are a sign of respect for those around us. Some people think good manners don't amount to much. They are wrong. The lack of manners repels people and signals that the offender considers himself superior to others or lacks the intelligence to know better.

Of course, the acts that reflect good manners sometimes change over time. No one today expects a man to throw his overcoat over a puddle to keep a woman's feet from getting wet, for example. The practice of opening a door for a woman has broadened to opening doors for everyone. Despite new versions of good manners that appear over time, their underlying basis remains the same: treat others with respect, and they will respond similarly. In business, good manners ease relations between opposing interests, making smoother transactions possible.

Final Thought

To some, I might seem old school, unwilling to adapt to the new century. While that may be true, it does not matter if I am the person with the authority to invest in your business, lend you money, give you a job, or buy your product. It is your responsibility and to your benefit to meet my expectations, not for me to meet yours.

PRINCIPLE 5

Look For Skills And Ability

"Never confuse education with intelligence."

— Unknown

Just because a person has a string of degrees behind their name doesn't mean that they are qualified to do a job. They may be well educated but lack what I call life or street smarts.

A person can have knowledge and lack the practical "know how" to put their knowledge into practice. They have the learning, but common sense may be missing. You should never assume that because a person is well educated that they have good life skills, critical thinking skills or can even move from point A to point B.

Ideally, I want people to work for me that have both book and life smarts; however, I have come to realize that quality isn't always confined to those with higher education. I never finished school myself. Most of us know someone with a long list of academic degrees who cannot fill a bucket with water during a thunderstorm. Conversely, neither Bill Gates of Microsoft or Steve Jobs of Apple graduated from college, but changed the world with their vision of what was possible. Thomas Edison turned night into day with a light bulb and without a formal education. John D. Rockefeller dominated the oil industry. John Glenn became a war hero and one of the most famous astronauts in history. None completed their education. Thousands have similar potential, but never get an opportunity due to the mistaken belief that a degree is proof of competence.

Would you rather work with a person without formal training who is hardworking, conscientious, and eager to learn or a degreed person who knows it all and considers his job as just a way to earn an income? I know that I would rather have a handful of employees that I could count on to do their best everyday than a warehouse full of workers who feel entitled and consider their work as just a job.

I had two employees work for me for over 40 years, "Bootsie" and James. These two men were hard workers, good people, and always courteous and respectful to the people around them. James had no formal education, but more common sense than most people you meet. He referred to his common sense as "mother's wit." If I had to choose between book-smarts and life smarts or "mother's it," I would take good old common sense any day. I would give a lot to have one more afternoon with either one of them as they are now deceased.

I don't mean to overlook people who have attended college and have degrees. Education is important and certainly there are many with degrees that also happen to have life smarts and good life skills also. However, many people without a college degree are just as capable as their more educated contemporaries. The school of hard knocks and life experience often teaches valuable lessons that can't be found anywhere else.

In fact, I would say that some of the best education you can get doesn't always come from a classroom. Once again, I am not putting down education. It's a great thing to get an education. However, it is equally true that people who have a skill, a trade or are good with their hands have much to offer and are needed in our world today.

If I had two people in my office applying for a position and one had a PhD and the other one had tremendous experience in a business or industry, which one would I hire? That would be a tough call. I might have to do a little more evaluation than just an interview. Just because someone doesn't have a string of degrees behind their name doesn't mean they don't have what it takes to be successful. They are just waiting for someone to believe in them and give them a chance to prove what they can do. When it comes to success, never underestimate the value of life skills, life smarts and on-the-job work experience.

PRINCIPLE 6

Employee Incentives Work

"People work for money but go the extra mile for recognition, praise and rewards."

— **Dale Carnegie**

Businesses struggle and fail because they can't keep good employees. It's a myth that employees leave companies. They don't leave the company, but their bosses. Every boss and manager should ask themselves, *"How do I keep good employees?"* and *"How do I encourage their commitment to the company?"*

I say, *"Take care of your people and they will take care of you."* It is a strategy I've always tried to follow, and I have yet to be disappointed with the result. Never think of people as a commodity. If you care about people and do good by them, people will respect you and will do good by you.

Recognize that quality labor is just as necessary as the money to fund a company. I would advise every owner and manager to treat your employees as your primary resource, or your business will always suffer. Invest in your people and consider people capital as important to have as financial capital.

One of every company's difficult challenges is keeping good employees. At the same time, I wanted each of my employees to have a shot at living the "American Dream" with extra income to provide savings for retirement. I learned that a firm commitment to incentive programs - sharing profits and bonuses - achieves both purposes.

Financial incentives create a change in attitude and increased personal commitment to the company. Employees appreciate management's faith in their abilities and willingly assume responsibility for their mutual success. As a result, everyone wins. The company reduces turnover costs and retains critical experience while employees make more money and have greater security.

Taking care of your employees is key for a successful business. I recommend three key strategies to increase production and performance:

2. Establish a fair profit-sharing incentive system...

I recommend that all businesses, whether commercial, wholesale, retail, or institutional, large or small, establish an incentive plan. Our plan was based on a realistic proforma financial statement for the operating year. Our projections were similar to the information we would give a bank to justify a loan - estimated sales, material costs, labor expense, and likely gross profits. In early December each year, we distributed annual bonuses equal to 10%-15% of earnings. That simple policy guaranteed that each employee had a very happy Christmas.

2. Develop a 2 + 2 hiring system...

For hiring and problem-solving, I introduced a formula for management to stay on track and have quality- and results-driven employees. The 2 plus 2 or the 2 minus 2 never fails!

Need a new employee? What do you do? I suggest you hire the best applicant you have on file. Don't be overly concerned whether or not you made the right choice because that is the beauty of the formula.

When a new employee starts, assign him or her the number 50. For the next ninety days, require a supervisor or personnel manager to rate the new employee's work performance daily. If it is acceptable, the rater adds two points to the cumulative total. If it doesn't meet expectations, the supervisor subtracts two points. At the end of ninety days, any new employee with eighty or more total points is kept. Any employee with under eighty points should be called into the office and released.

This method of evaluation never fails. If you are serious about solving a personnel problem, never compromise your decision. This simple formula can also be used to solve a lot of other issues.

In addition to the scoring system, I used constant reminders to keep my employees motivated. I posted management notes on the entrance to the plant for all employees and visitors to read:

Let me give you an actual example of how incentives worked for my first company's employees to increase employee morale and production. In our first year, we employed 25 workers. Our annual net sales for that year were $4 million. Our projected labor expense was 21.5% of net sales or $861,000. The actual labor cost was $750,000, which left approximately $111,000 for bonuses or $4,440 per employee. The average wage that year was $30,000. Each payment of $4,440 represented earnings increases of almost 15%. The company's net profit was $800,000, equal to a profit margin of 20% of the net sales; the national average profit margin for companies of similar size in the industry was 6%. I know that the incentive program played a big part in our bottom line and greater than expected earnings increase.

3. Put Experienced Employees in Charge…

One of the things I did in each of my businesses was to put employees in charge of the plant. I eliminated all supervisory positions and titles except for the plant manager. Instead of keeping employees whose job was to watch other employees, each department was managed by a senior, experienced employee working alongside the other workers in that department. For their extra clerical duties and time, they received a 10% larger annual bonus than the other employees. This change gave the employees a sense of ownership in the business and an extra incentive to make the company successful.

Respecting Your Employees

Fairly compensated employees are less likely to be attracted to an outside labor organization as I learned while managing a field job in Tampa, Florida.

The company had won a bid to construct several large diesel fuel storage tanks for Seaboard Railroad. When we moved to the job site, a union representative for the local steelworkers confronted me. He demanded that each worker pay his Union $100 to work on the job. Like many of his ilk, the representative was a belligerent bully, used to getting his way. At the time, I knew this extra expense wasn't going to allow us to take the job and would cost my men much needed work. I later learned that the railroad had a union agreement requiring the use of union labor on all construction jobs.

Knowing that our bid had not included an allowance for the extra cost, I referred him to Johnny Ramsey, one of our workers standing nearby. Johnny was a hard worker, popular with the others on the crew, and one of the most independent people I knew. A physical specimen with incredible natural strength, I suspected the meeting between Johnny and the union man would be quite entertaining.

The union representative walked up to Johnny and opened the conversation with a blunt demand for $100 in union fees from each man on the crew. He threatened that any worker who refused to pay would be photographed and would not be able to work on any future union jobs.

Johnny stared at the representative a few moments, then told him, "*Go get your camera and take your pictures. When you take mine, I am going to shove that* *camera down your throat to your navel, and then I am going to give you my $100."* The union man stepped back and slowly walked away. I never saw him again, or any other union representative for the next three months as we completed the contract. At the time, I was just looking out for my employees.

PRINCIPLE 7

Don't Run From Risks

"You can run with the big dogs or sit on the porch and bark."

— **Wallace Arnold**

Sometimes you must step out of your comfort zone and take a risk to discover your own true talents and abilities. Fear of failure keeps many people from ever realizing their potential. People are often given opportunities that are outside of their expertise or experience at the time, but do not take advantage of them due to fear.

I learned that nothing is gained by playing it safe all of the time. Sometimes, you have to take risks to experience a greater measure of success. You just do. I did, and my decision changed the course of my career. One opportunity after another followed - chances for bigger jobs, more recognition, and larger paychecks.

As a young man, my willingness to weld white metal at a Paper Mill in South Carolina led to another experience which got written up in an article in a national trade magazine. When a twelve-foot in diameter, two-foot-wide, two-ton drive wheel for the plant's only debarking machine shattered, four of us (two welders and two helpers) worked twenty-five hours straight on the repair, resting only for bathroom breaks, snacks, and changing out the gas cylinders for the four acetylene torches. More than two hundred pounds of bronze welding rods were needed to complete the job. The project - a monumental task completed in just over a single day - drew the trade journal publisher's interest and the complimentary publicity.

Like many young men of my generation, I joined the Army during WWII. Learning of my experience with white metal, the Army sent me to ordinance service in a heavy automotive maintenance battalion. For the next four years, I worked in parts manufacturing and attended classes in mechanical, industrial, and combustion engineering. I will never forget an instructor's answer to a question about awarding a certificate to prove our attendance: *"The training you are getting is both theoretical and practical. One day you will have engineers working for you that have masters degrees."*

During the Battle of the Bulge, my battalion was ordered to report to the front lines in Belgium. I was the only one of nine hundred men who did not go and it was a huge disappointment for me at the time. I subsequently learned that my exception had been ordered by a general who saw a zinc die for truck repair that I had made. In my disappointment with being left behind, I didn't realize that the experiences and training I received were preparing me for my future work in the steel industry. Sometimes, what we think is a presently a setback could be a setup for something greater in the future. Hindsight is always 20/20. I can see that now, but I sure couldn't see it back then. Maybe, if I had gone to the front lines with my buddies, I wouldn't be here to write this book.

After my release from the service, I returned to the paper mill before accepting a job as an erection superintendent in field construction for a large steel manufacturing and fabrication firm in Norfolk, Virginia. In 1955, I left that company to build my own steel fabricating company that ultimately employed 150 workers. The company was named Eastern Steel Products Corporation and was located in Rocky Mount, North Carolina.

During this time, my business was featured in a newspaper write up in the *News and Observer* newspaper of Raleigh, North Carolina. The title of the article was "Young Industrialists Team to Form Successful Business at Rocky Mount." The article was written by Bill Womble. Here is my synopsis of the article…

"Williams and Garrison teamed up together in late 1954 to go into the highly competitive metals business. After setting up shop with limited capital in January 1955, the young industrialists didn't wait for business to come to them. About that time, liquid fertilizers were booming. The two men designed and built new types of tanks to handling the popular fertilizers. Williams and Garrison continued to look for new business, taking every kind of metals job that came their way including fire trucks, specialized steel buildings for Uncle Sam, bulk tanks to store various chemicals, and a new plant to produce fertilizer. One of their unusual projects was the design and manufacture of amphibious houseboats.

The company is especially adept in designing and making tools that are not available or too expensive for the small company. For example, when the company needed an automatic aluminum-welder to build aluminum tanks, Garrison designed and built his own for a fraction of the $15,000 cost of a new one. Since the machine was used solely by and in the Eastern plant, there were no patent issues or costs.

Garrison says the most unusual job they've had was a Civil Aeronautics Authority contract for 105 Vortac stations, the electronic system scattered throughout the county to aid pilot navigation. Each station costs about $40,000. Garrison and Williams only heard about the contract to construct sixty-two stations two days before bids were due. Working around the clock and mostly in the dark, the partners submitted a winning bid, just $15 under the next bidder. *"Sheer luck, I guess,"* Garrison said. Before the end of the initial contract, the CAA added forty-three additional stations to the order for a total of one hundred five. Garrison reported that the firm did *"very well [financially] on the contract."*

The Eastern Steel Products venture taught me that success requires equal parts seeking opportunities and also creating them for yourself. The old expression of nothing ventured, nothing gained is so true. Some of my decisions were made without really being confident of the outcome. But, whether in life or business, you won't know until you try. How can you have success if you are not willing to step out of your comfort zone, take risks, and try new things?

PRINCIPLE 8

Confront Problems Head-On

"All problems become smaller if you don't dodge them, but confront them."

— **William Halsey**

In 1963, I was hired to manage two investor-owned plants in Richmond, Virginia. Both companies happened to be on the same property. One was a decorative chrome plating plant that refinished automobile bumpers. The second plant was a hot-dip galvanizing plant. Both companies were approximately two years old and had never made a profit. The investors needed help to get out of the red, so the monetary offer to me was quite generous: an excellent salary plus one-third of the annual profits of both plants. Accepting the job was a challenge for me since I had no experience in either metal plating or galvanizing. Talk about stepping out of one's comfort zone!

In the first three months, I concentrated my time on improving the plating operation since I felt it had the most potential for immediate financial recovery. The company had sales of approximately 250 bumpers per day. However, output was only 65 to 70 units daily, far below its capacity. After implementing a time study in each department, I changed from an hourly pay compensation plan to an incentive program tied to the production per piece in each department. At the end of three months, production had increased to approximately 240 units per day. I eliminated twenty-five excessive payroll slots and increased the remaining employees' pay by an average of 20%.

After three months, I turned my attention to the galvanizing plant. The business had lost most of its customers due to poor customer service and low-quality work. Morale was low and work discipline was non-existent. I knew radical change was required - breaking old habits and instilling a pride of ownership in the employees - and I was determined to be the change agent.

One Friday evening, I held a group meeting with the galvanizing plant employees. I opened the meeting with a warning, *"I notice that some of you do not even tie your shoelaces at work. Some of you take sunbaths or spend most of the day leaning against the columns in the yard yakking when you should be working. Beginning Monday morning at 8 a.m., this attitude will not be tolerated. If you plan to work here and help make this company successful, come back Monday. Otherwise, do not come back."*

Only one employee showed up that Monday, a bookkeeper who worked in the plant building office. That morning, I asked to see his accounting records. I discovered that he had drawn lines in many entries instead of numbers.

I told him, *"You do not keep books with lines, but with numbers. When you leave work today, do not return."* He replied, *"I admire you for your effort, but this company will never operate profitably."* *"Time will tell,"* I thought.

What a great way to begin a turnaround with no experience in galvanizing and no employees. Those kind of circumstances will get you moving, if nothing else will. My first action was to ask two brothers from the plating plant (I knew to be good workers) if they wanted to learn how to galvanize. They said, *"Why not?"* Interestingly, one of those men went on to work for me for the next 42 years.

The number one problem in both plants was a lack of material handling equipment and not the coating or plating processes. I made phone calls throughout Virginia and North Carolina to fabricators who knew me personally. With their help, I was able to restart the galvanizing operations. Over the following three months, we installed all new material handling equipment, paved the yard for storing incoming material, and hired new employees. I initially transferred workers who I trusted from the plating operation to the galvanizing plant. But, because sales had dropped so severely, I didn't need a lot of employees initially. Several months later, both plants were actually earning profits with excellent profit margins and that continued during my time there, leaving in 1976.

Many managers have difficulty with confrontational meetings. Either they don't like conflict or they are optimists and do not understand why anyone would shirk their responsibilities. Consequently, when performance is less than needed or expected, they dilute or sugarcoat the bad news and no improvement occurs.

Some managers simply don't like confrontations and will go to extreme lengths to avoid them. They hope the issue will correct itself over time. In my career, Pollyanna thinking never works, molehills become mountains and more difficult to resolve. I've always thought that correcting someone's poor work habits, requiring their best effort, or insisting that their work meets high standards was a favor to them. While criticism should never be cruelly delivered, honest appraisals are expected by every person who wants to improve. Those who can't accept correction are bad apples and need to be dismissed before they ruin the entire workforce culture.

One of my first management jobs was in a company division that made gasoline tank trailers for major oil companies. When I reported for work the first morning, I walked through the building to get acquainted with the products and the manufacturing process. Scanning the unfinished tanks, I noticed the skirts intended to support the under-cabinet of the trailer were not evenly positioned on each side of the elliptically shaped tank.

Even a novice like me knew the work would not meet expected requirements, so I asked the man in charge how long he had been doing that work. When he said, "*15 years,*" I asked him why he didn't know how to position the skirts correctly. He did not take my question kindly and let me know of his displeasure. I told him to clock out and take 30 days off. I also suggested that when he returned, maybe he would have a better attitude and get the work done correctly. After the other employees saw the result of our disagreement, I had no problem with employee cooperation. I worked in that department for an additional two years from 1949 through 1951.

The best way to handle problems is never to run from them and to deal with them head-on. Tolerating sloppy work habits does no one any favors.

PRINCIPLE 9

Stay Humble

"The best laid plans of mice and men often run awry."

— **Robert Burns**

Lack of Knowledge

In 1962, I was hired to manage a manufacturing plant in Virginia to fabricate pier cones for the Chesapeake Bay Bridge and all the air ducts for the tunnel sections. This was a monumental job and required approximately 300 employees to be involved in this contract.

In addition, we also had a contract to build a $50,000 pressure vessel. The specifications required plastic paint that I had no experience with whatsoever. We tried a mineral paint thinner, but could not produce a smooth finish. No one in the plant knew what the problem was. It was during a management meeting with the president of the company that he told me, *"You don't know what the problem is because you don't know what the problem is."*

I thought he was completely crazy, but after thinking about it, I knew he was right. Soon afterward, we sought the advice of a chemist who prescribed the correct thinner for the paint - methyl ethyl ketone - that solved our problem. The moral of this story is to not attempt to do any job without doing research or consulting with a key person who has the correct education or knowledge. Too many people waste time and resources because they think they know a solution without knowing the problem.

Businesses fail because those in charge lack proper knowledge and planning experience. I suspect that 75% of business failures result from a lack of knowledge for the job. Consequently, managers begin a cycle of trial and error, wasting time and resources. Never be too proud to ask for help. If you don't know something, ask someone who does know.

Misplaced Confidence

Keeping a humble attitude is important because success sometimes leads to pride and false confidence in one's abilities. One of my proudest accomplishments at Eastern Steel Products was the design and construction of AMPHIB-A-HOME... an amphibious, unsinkable houseboat for use on both land and water. This structure met the government's highway standards and Coast Guard requirements for water.

The boat hull was a steel channel frame made from 13-gauge high tensile steel. Turning a hand crank would drop and retract the wheel assembly into the hull. A rectangular-shaped cabin constructed with four-inch thick Styrofoam panels, four feet wide and eight-foot-long, attached to the hull made the 3,700-

pound vessel slightly more than the weight of a 1955 Chevrolet Bel Air automobile.

Quarter-inch thick mahogany veneer covered the interior surfaces while thin-gauge decorative aluminum metal protected the exterior surfaces. The cabin roof, accessed by a metal ladder, served as a sun deck. Metal railing protected visitors from accidentally falling into the water from the boat's front and back decks.

The cabin, designed to accommodate four people, included four screened windows, six port windows, an aluminum door, and rear deck storage. We designed each boat with comfort and utility in mind with C.G. lighting, a porcelain sink (with a chrome faucet), a 20-gallon water tank, a hot water heater, ample cupboard space, and a refrigerator with a 50-pound icebox. A two-burner propane stove, a great toilet, a dining table, four innerspring beds, and a closet with a full-length mirror was standard in each unit. Powered by a 50-horsepower outboard motor, owners or guests could steer the boat with a conventional steering apparatus.

We licensed retail dealers in several states and Canada to sell the craft for $5,000, plus the cost of the motor. We then embarked on a marketing campaign, taking our houseboat to boat shows across the country. Once at the North Carolina State Fair, we hired an upcoming duo to sing a few songs from the deck of the vessel to attract attention. They were the Everly Brothers, who became famous with the songs "Bye Bye Love", "Wake Up Little Susie", and others.

At a Chicago boat show, our craft won 1st prize for its unique design. A national company, Ballard Flour, awarded the prize and printed a full-page ad for several weeks featuring the boat in the Sunday newspapers across the east coast. We gave away one of our houseboats on *Bid and Buy*, a nationally syndicated television show in Chicago.

We knew we had a great boat that was totally unique in its design. Our enthusiasm seemed justified as we received thousands of sales inquiries. Unfortunately, interest does not always result in sales. In fact, we had very few sales, even though I was quite proud of our creation and was confident we would have great success. We didn't.

In retrospect, I realize that we made several mistakes in our decision to pursue the houseboat market. Just because you think it is a good idea doesn't mean it is what your customers want. For example, we were sure that the quality of our boats was the highest on the market and would attract buyers even at a higher price.

Boat manufacturers in the mid-1950s were turning to cheap fiberglass structures, replacing steel and wood. Though less durable or as strong as steel, fiberglass could be molded in a wide variety of colors. As a consequence, AMPHIB-A-HOME, with its higher quality and durability, was more expensive than its competitors. To me, a fiberglass houseboat compared to our houseboat was the difference between fool's gold and 24-karat gold.

Because we didn't understand the consumer market for boats at the time nor what consumers were looking for, we over-valued the quality component of our product and its impact on retail prices.

Success doesn't just come automatically from good ideas. After selling Eastern Steel products in NC in

1960, I also invested in a barbecue business in South Carolina that sold product to grocery stores statewide. We had a great start and an initial demand for the product. At the time, I thought it was a good idea, but the North Carolina-style barbecue wasn't received well in South Carolina. The moral of this story is that a product that sells well in one state doesn't mean it will be accepted well in another state. Demand and timing are everything in business.

The business principle we learned from our houseboat venture and barbecue restaurant was, "Stay humble." No one can claim a 100% success rate in all they do, even though they take the right steps. In real life, unexpected circumstances can suddenly turn markets and plans upside down as we discovered in the 1973 Arab oil embargo, the financial crisis of 2008-2009, and the recent coronavirus pandemic of 2019-2020.

PRINCIPLE 10

Never Give Up

"Winners never quit and quitters never win."

— Vince Lombardi

After continual frustration with the owner of the galvanizing and plating plants, I decided it was time to venture out on my own again. I was in mid-life and I knew it was risky. I also knew I couldn't stay there and be continually frustrated with the owner and his lack of wisdom in business decisions. So, I left my management position and decided to step out and start my own galvanizing plant.

In 1977, I approached a banker for loan to construct a new 20,000 square foot galvanizing plant that would open as Virginia Galvanizing. I knew a little about investments and risks, but applying for that loan was one of the most unusual bank meetings that I ever experienced. The vice president in charge of industrial loans came to my house on a Sunday afternoon. He began the conversation with the suggestion that I think twice about borrowing the money. He cautioned me to not put everything I owned in jeopardy to build this new plant. He warned me that if this venture didn't work, I would probably never again have any net worth.

I thanked him for his concern, then told him that, 17 years earlier, I had lost everything I owned. I made an unwise investment in the restaurant industry. I told him that going broke before 40 was a valuable learning experience for me. I had learned that there is more to this life than money. I also shared that I had already signed a contract to build the new plant and I planned to have it in operation by the middle of the year. He seemed especially shocked when I told him that the new plant will be different from other galvanizing facilities with only a plant manager and no supervisors. My employees would operate the plant and would benefit or lose from its success. I expressed my conviction that employee morale and production would be extraordinarily high since they would have skin in the game with me.

The long and short of our meeting was the bank loaned me the money. While most plants of that size take a minimum of a year to build, we worked 15-hour days and completed it in four months. Virginia Galvanizing was the first hot-dip galvanizing plant in central Virginia. We also introduced the first full-length kettle preheater and patented instant-heat combustion for the hot-dip galvanizing industry in North America.

Using a preheat system before the hot-dip process allowed us to do some unusual things. For example, we galvanized the "Four Horseman" sculpture at the entrance of Regent University in Virginia Beach, Virginia. Our preheat system ensured that the individual pieces were free of moisture and prevented instant heat expansion when they were dipped in 850 degrees of molten zinc. I am incredibly proud of that accomplishment since that sculpture had been designed and carefully created by a gifted female artist over a two-year period.

The plant specialized in spin galvanizing using the patented revolutionary Spin-A-Batch™ centrifuge I developed when managing the Richmond Virginia galvanizing plant. I patented Spin-A-Batch™ and licensed its manufacture and marketing worldwide in 1970. It continues to be sold globally today. Before I invented Spin-A-Batch™, no centrifuge anywhere in the world could spin more than 50 pounds in a single basket load. Centrifuges were floor-based and with a housing for a 13-inch basket that was powered by an electric motor. A weight exceeding 50 pounds would cause the centrifuge to turn on its side with any sudden thrust of power.

I designed a suspension to eliminate the thrust problem and allowing the basket to spin freely. There were four different models, each able to spin 1,000 pounds or more for each series. Before the introduction of Spin-A-Batch™, normal spinning loads were limited to less than 1,000 pounds. With the new centrifuge, our production significantly increased. My unique centrifuge revolutionized the galvanizing industry.

The latest model 4000 series centrifuge is still being sold today for $38,000 per unit. While it is a sizable investment, it will pay for itself in approximately three months in labor savings. In my opinion, the average galvanizing plant using this Spin-A-Batch™ centrifuge can increase their earnings by a minimum of $200,000 a year from lower labor costs and increased efficiency.

When I started Virginia Galvanizing, I will admit that I had many nights of poor sleep. I would wake up at 2 a.m., wet with sweat, wondering if I could meet the payment schedule the next day. But I was always honest with the bankers and they believed in me. We paid back that seven-year loan in only three years in

1980. Jack Kelly, my attorney, once told me that the bankers thought I walked on water. A real compliment for sure.

The company continued to prosper. Ten years after paying off the loan, I paid federal and state income taxes of $503,285.00 for a single year (1990).

I sold that company in 2007 to finally spend more time with my family and friends. However, my Spin-A-Batch™ system is still being sold around the world today.

Bonus: Necessity is the Mother of Invention

I've always heard that "necessity is the mother of invention." How true. Most inventions and products come into being because of a need. In my career, I mostly invented things because of an interest or a problem that needed solving. Since 1956, I have patented six unique inventions through my company Garrison Industries, Inc. (or its subsidiaries) covering the United States and industrial nations worldwide.

Three-wheel Trailer for Anhydrous Ammonia

My first invention was a trailer for hauling anhydrous ammonia to a farmer's fields. The patent was granted because the running gear, the rear axles for the wheels, and the front single-wheel assembly was welded directly to a 265 psi pressure tank. The trailer was legal for interstate highway travel.

We introduced the NI-TRAILER, primarily aluminum tanks mounted on three-wheel trailers by a frame to hold them on a solid rear axle. Our first order for the trailer was 1,000 units. But, when liquid nitrogen took the place of anhydrous ammonia a year later, we discontinued the line.

AMPHIB-A-HOME

My second patent, issued in 1958, was the amphibious, unsinkable houseboat that I discussed in the chapter titled "Principle 9: Stay Humble".

Spin-A-Batch™

My third, fourth, fifth, and sixth U.S patents were for a revolutionary portable pneumatic centrifuge called Spin-A-Batch™ that revolutionized hot-dip galvanizing. The subsequent patents were issued for significant innovations that expanded the utility of the centrifuge.

Ladder Secure

My seventh and most recent invention was a life-saving base used to stabilize and support extension ladders. Though I have not sought a patent, I did register Ladder Secure Inc with the american trademark office. My interest in developing a safer solution for ladder use followed the loss of a good friend thrown to the ground by an extension ladder slipping from its base.

In my research, I discovered that more than 40,000 lives had been lost the previous year in the U.S. alone. To my surprise, more fatalities and injuries are caused by accidents using extension ladders than the use of other tools combined. I designed a base with parts that attached securely to the ladder and tested it for over five years. The product enables a user to stand the ladder upright, in and outdoors, without fear of the ladder slipping in any direction.

Unfortunately, I did not receive a patent for my work, making any financial success impossible since anyone could freely copy my design. I did have some comfort when my patent attorney told me that only 3% of all inventions worldwide ever reach the marketplace.

Bonus: James and Bootsie

I would like to pay special tribute to two employees who worked for me for over 30 years, James Hespeth and Charles Carter (known as "Bootsie"). They performed their tasks without compromise, enriching my life more than any monetary benefit I ever received.

In 1972, I purchased approximately 88 acres of land in Mechanicsville, Virginia, to build a 7,000 square foot southern colonial home on around 5 acres of the property. I needed help maintaining our home site, the many acres of grass, and a par 4 golf fairway and green. I recruited James and Bootsie to help.

James passed away in 1982, followed by Charles in 1994, and I would forfeit everything I own to see either of these men for only one minute. I have had many great mentors in my life, but I learned so much from these men.

James Hespeth moved to Virginia from North Carolina in the 1950s. He had very little formal education, but, without a doubt, more common sense than most people. He also worked for me in the galvanizing plant. He never called me by my real name, always "Cap'n" and was a very comical man.

I picked up James and Bootsie each morning and fed them breakfast. One morning just a few months before James passing, he had difficulty getting into my vehicle. He explained that a friend had given him some homemade wine. *"It tasted so good that I couldn't stop drinking it,"* he said. *"Cap'n, please don't tell Mrs. Garrison about this because you don't fool with God, you know."* To this day, I think about that and have a good chuckle.

He told me many wise things. One piece of advice that I will never forget was, *"Cap'n, you look like you are trying to be in two places at the same time. And if you keep this up, you will end up one place and stay there."* I remember his words to stay on the straight and narrow, *"Cap'n, don't ever look down and don't ever look back. Keep looking up to your Heavenly Father when you need help."* Or, one of my favorites of all time, *"Cap'n, don't worry about the mule going blind, just load the wagon."* Every time I think about it I smile and the wisdom is profound.

Bootsie and I were very close too. He once purchased a pickup truck from a dealer who knew us both well. I had no idea Bootsie needed a truck so I was very surprised when a dealer called me about the truck he was purchasing. The dealer asked Bootsie how he wanted to pay for the truck, and his response was, *"He'll give you a check."* When the dealer called and told me the story, I had a big laugh and wrote the check.

Epilogue

Life affords us many opportunities. If we are open to them and the people that God puts in our path, we can learn so much. It was true in my life and I believe it can be true in yours as well. I have always said that this day like all days are good if we know what to do with them. They really are.

If you want to be successful in life or business, you have to work hard, take risks, and even be willing to fail. I have always said, *"Strive for the impossible in order to achieve what is necessary."* When someone told me it couldn't be done, that was generally fuel for me to find a way to do it. The fact is, if you don't get off the porch, you can't ever really win at anything. Nothing ventured is nothing gained.

Of course, do your homework, your planning, and even find a good mentor. Ultimately, you have to take action and be willing to take a risk. The more you are willing to step out of your comfort zone in life or business, the more likely you are to achieve success. Interestingly, a law of physics points out that an object in motion tends to stay in motion. So, get moving.

Regardless of your economic or educational status, success can come when you work hard, are determined, and dare to achieve great things. It happened for others. It certainly happened for me and I believe it can happen for you also!

Note:

Contributions from the sales of this book will be made to the Shriners' Hospital for Children.

www.ingramcontent.com/pod-product-compliance
Lightning Source LLC
Chambersburg PA
CBHW071423210526
45465CB00001B/505